DISCIPLESHIP EXPLORED

STUDY GUIDE

Copyright © 2009 Christianity Explored
www.christianityexplored.org

Published by
The Good Book Company
Tel (UK): 0845 225 0880
Tel (int) + (44) 208 942 0880
Email: admin@thegoodbook.co.uk

Websites
UK & Europe: www.thegoodbook.co.uk
N America: www.thegoodbook.com
Australia: www.thegoodbook.com.au
New Zealand: www.thegoodbook.co.nz

ISBN Universal Edition 9781906334840
ISBN International Student Edition 9781906334895

All rights reserved. No part of this publication may be reproduced, stored in a retrieval system, or transmitted in any form or by any means, electronic, mechanical, photocopying, recording or otherwise, without the prior permission of the publisher or a licence permitting restricted copying.

In the UK such licences are issued by the Copyright Licensing Agency, 90 Tottenham Court Road, London W1P 9HE. BRITISH LIBRARY CATALOGUING IN PUBLICATION DATA. A catalogue record for this book is available from the British Library.

Unless otherwise stated, Scripture quotations are taken from the HOLY BIBLE, NEW INTERNATIONAL VERSION Copyright © 1973, 1978, 1984 by the International Bible Society.

Used by permission of Hodder and Stoughton Limited. All rights reserved.

Grateful thanks to: Paul Chelson, Barry Cooper, Steve Devane, Kerry Fee, Alison Mitchell, Andre Parker, Sam Shammas, Tim Thornborough, Nicole Wagner Carter and Anne Woodcock, and the many others who contributed to the development of the Discipleship Explored Universal Edition and International Student Edition.

Design by The Good Book Company

Printed in China

	Before We Begin	4
Week 1	**How can I be sure I'm a Christian?** Philippians 1:1-11	5
Week 2	**What am I living for?** Philippians 1:12-26	9
Week 3	**Together for Christ?** Philippians 1:27 – 2:11	13
Week 4	**How should I live for Christ?** Philippians 2:5-18	17
Week 5	**Can I be good enough for God?** Philippians 3:1-9	21
Week 6	**How can I know Christ better?** Philippians 3:10 – 4:1	25
Week 7	**How can I rejoice in Christ?** Philippians 4:2-9	29
Week 8	**How can I be content in Christ?** Philippians 4:10-23	33
Extra	**An example to follow?** Philippians 2:19-30	37

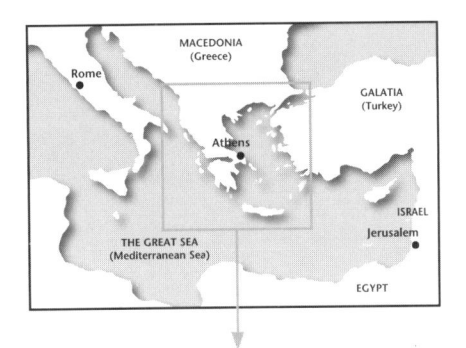

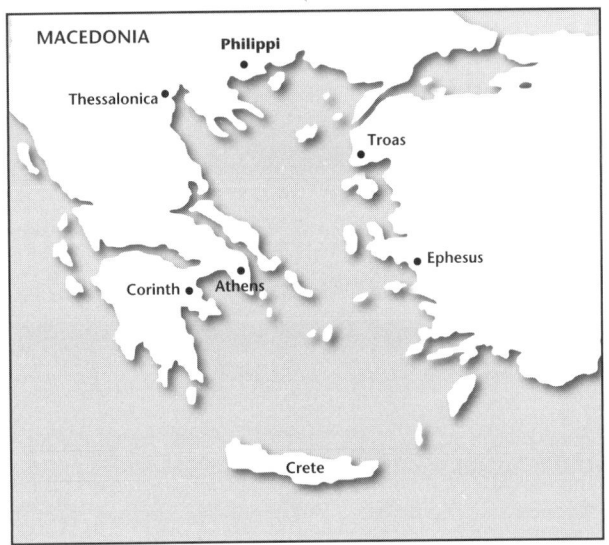

Before we begin

Welcome to Discipleship Explored!

These Bible studies look at a letter from the New Testament. It was written by Paul to a group of Christians living in the city of Philippi. Philippi was a Roman colony in ancient Greece.

Paul and Timothy visited Philippi to tell people about Jesus. You can read about what happened there in Acts 16. They were forced to leave after a short time because the city rulers did not want them to tell people about Jesus or cause any trouble. They left behind them a small group of new Christians. Paul wrote this letter to them from prison in Rome. He wanted to:

- Encourage the new Christians in Philippi
- Help them keep going as Christians in difficult times
- Remind them about the good news of Jesus Christ
- Give them practical instructions on what it means to live as a follower of Christ. That is what the word disciple means – a learner, a follower.

You may have recently made a decision to become a Christian. You may be someone who is still thinking about what it means to follow Jesus. Or you may be someone who has been a Christian for years, and want to go over the basics once again.

Whoever you are, this short letter will help you understand how good it is to be a follower of Jesus Christ, and how he calls his disciples to live for him today.

Philippians 1:1–11

Week 1

How can I be sure I'm a Christian?

This letter to the Philippian Christians was written from someone in prison.

■ **What would you write to your friends if you were unfairly put in prison?**

_____

_____

Read Philippians 1:1–11

Read the verses again. Are there any words you do not understand? Look at the Bible words list on the next page to help you.

Read Philippians 1:1–2

Verse 1 is like the envelope of the letter. It shows who it is from and who it is going to.

1 Who is the letter from and who was it sent to?

_____

_____

WHO WAS PAUL?

Paul was originally called Saul. As a devoted Jew, he hated the first Jewish Christians and put many of them in prison. But while travelling to Damascus, he was stopped by a bright light and heard Jesus Christ speaking to him. This experience changed Paul completely. He became a Christian and was sent by Jesus to be a teacher and leader. You can read this story in Acts chapter 9.

Paul travelled a lot around Southern Europe and Asia telling others about Jesus Christ. He organised the new disciples into churches, and wrote letters to them, teaching them and encouraging them to keep going. He was often persecuted himself, and was eventually executed by the Romans. Many of Paul's letters are now in the New Testament. Philippians is one of them.

2 What does Paul say about himself and Timothy?

3 What does Paul call the readers of the letter?

Read Philippians 1:3–8

4 How does Paul feel about the Philippian Christians? Why?

"Partnership in the gospel" means that the Philippian Christians were working with Paul to tell other people about Jesus.

5 What is Paul confident about in verse 6?

BIBLE WORDS

v1 Christ. This name means "the chosen king". The same word in Hebrew is "Messiah". There are many promises in the Old Testament about the Christ/Messiah. They show that he would be God's chosen king.

v1 saints. Holy ones; those who God has set apart for himself. Every Christian is a saint.

v1 overseers and deacons. Church leaders.

v2 grace. God's gift of forgiveness to people who do not deserve it.

v2 peace. Peace with God.

v2 Lord. Master.

v5 gospel. The good news about Jesus Christ.

v6 day of Christ. The day when Jesus Christ will return to judge the world. (See verse 10 also.)

v7 confirming. Showing something is true.

v8 testify. Be a witness. A witness tells others the truth about something that they have seen or heard.

6 Is becoming a Christian an "inside change" or an "outside change"? Who makes the change? Why is it important to understand this?

The "inside change" of becoming a Christian can be seen in an "outside change".

7 What "outside changes" showed Paul that God had begun his work in the Philippians (verse 5)?

8 Have you ever been unsure that you are a real Christian? What made you feel that way?

9 Have you seen any "outside changes" in your life since you became a Christian? What are they?

BIBLE WORDS

v8 I long for all of you. I want to be with you.

v8 with the affection of Christ Jesus. With the love of Jesus.

v9 abound. Increase.

v9 insight. Being able to understand something clearly.

v10 discern. Understand or judge correctly.

v10 pure and blameless. Someone who does not think wrong things or do wrong things.

v11 fruit. Results.

v11 righteousness. Goodness that is good enough for God. You must be perfect and have no sin to be good enough for God. Jesus Christ is the only person who has ever been perfect.

Read Philippians 1:9-11

Paul knows that the Philippians, like all Christians, are not perfect. So he prays for them.

10 What does Paul pray for and why?

_____

_____

_____

11 What does Paul hope will be the result of this (see verses 10-11)?

_____

_____

12 Paul's prayer can help us to pray for other Christians and ourselves. What should we thank God for, and what should we ask him to do in our lives?

_____

_____

■ *Pray these things now for yourself and others.*

THINGS TO PRAY FOR

MEMORY VERSE

"He who began a good work in you will carry it on to completion until the day of Christ Jesus."

Philippians 1:6

Philippians 1:12–26

What am I living for?

Week 2

■ Tell the group three things that make you happy.

_____
_____

Read Philippians 1:12-26

Read the verses again. Are there any words you do not understand? Look at the Bible words list on the next page to help you.

Read Philippians 1:12-18a

1 What makes Paul happy (verse 18)? What is most important to him?

_____
_____

SUMMARY OF WEEK 1

◁ Paul wrote this letter to a group of new Christians living in the city of Philippi to help them keep going as Christians.

◁ We know that God has begun his good work in us if we are living as partners in the gospel, and want to obey Jesus Christ more and more.

◁ We can be confident that whatever happens God will finish the work of salvation that he has begun.

◁ We mustn't depend on how good we feel or don't feel; instead we can trust in what God has done for us in Jesus Christ.

◁ God helps us to grow in love, knowledge and understanding so that we can live in a way that honours God, until the day when Jesus Christ returns.

9

2 Read verses 12-14 again. Where is Paul? Why is he there?

_____

_____

3 Many people think being in prison is a disaster. What does Paul think (see verses 12-14)?

_____

_____

4 What surprises you about verses 15-18 and why?

_____

_____

5 Have you, or someone you know, experienced opposition because you are a Christian?

_____

_____

6 Paul experienced opposition because of his faith. How does Paul's example help us to think differently about the opposition we will face?

_____

_____

BIBLE WORDS

v12 brothers. Christians. All Christians are part of God's family.

v12 gospel. The message (good news) about Jesus Christ.

v12 advance the gospel. Help more people understand the message about Jesus.

v14 encouraged. Become more confident.

v14 courageously. Bravely.

v15 preach Christ. Explain who Christ is and what he has done for us on the cross; tell the gospel.

v15 envy. Wanting what belongs to other people.

v15 rivalry. Competing against other people because you want to be the best.

v16 the latter. The people mentioned second (in verse 15).

v17 the former. The people mentioned first (in verse 15).

v17 selfish ambition. Wanting to make yourself more important than other people.

Read Philippians 1:18b–26

7 Who helps Paul (verse 19)?

_____

_____

8 What does Paul think about his death? Why? (See verses 21-23.)

_____

_____

_____

9 Why does Paul choose life instead of death (see verses 22-26)?

_____

_____

_____

10 How would your friends finish this sentence: "For me to live is…"

_____

BIBLE WORDS

v17 sincerely. Honestly.

v18 motives. Reasons.

v18 I rejoice. I am joyful (very happy).

v19 The Spirit of Jesus Christ. The Holy Spirit. God sends his Holy Spirit to help people who become Christians.

v19 deliverance. Salvation (not rescue from prison, but being saved by God, from sin, death and judgment).

v20 eagerly. Very much.

v20 sufficient. Enough.

v20 exalted. Honoured.

v21 gain. Something better.

v22 fruitful labour. Hard work that gets good results.

v23 torn between. Can't decide between two things.

v23 depart. Leave.

v25 progress. Growth.

v25 the faith. Your relationship with God.

v26 on account of. Because of.

- How would you finish the same sentence? "For me to live is..."

11 Paul says in verse 21: "To live is Christ and to die is gain". What does he mean?

12 Look again at what Paul thinks about his own suffering – verses 12, 18a & 21. What does this teach us about praying for Christians who are suffering for the gospel?

13 God does not promise us easy lives when we become Christians. What have we learned that will help us when we suffer for the gospel?

■ *Share with the rest of the group things you would like to pray for.*
■ *Pray especially for those who are suffering for their faith. Pray they would know the confidence that Paul has.*

THINGS TO PRAY FOR

MEMORY VERSE

"For to me, to live is Christ and to die is gain."

Philippians 1:21

Philippians 1:27 – 2:11

Together for Christ?

Week 3

■ Talk about a team or group you have enjoyed being a member of.

_____
_____
_____

Read aloud Philippians 1:27 – 2:11

Read the verses again. Are there any words you do not understand? Look at the Bible words list on the next page to help you.

Read Philippians 1:27–30

1 How does Paul want the Philippian Christians to behave (see verse 27a)?

_____
_____
_____

SUMMARY OF WEEKS 1-2

◁ Paul wrote this letter to a group of new Christians living in Philippi to help them keep going as Christians.

◁ Paul was confident that whatever happens God would finish the work of salvation that he began in them. Therefore we can have the same confidence.

◁ The most important thing in Paul's life was that people were hearing about Jesus.

◁ Paul teaches the Philippians (and us) that: "To live is Christ and to die is gain." (1:21) Everything we do should come from a desire to see Jesus become better known and honoured by others. We can be joyful when we face opposition. Christians can look forward to death because it is the doorway to new life with Christ.

"To stand firm in one spirit" and *"contend as one man for the faith of the gospel"* (verse 27) means to all stay sure of what they believe, and work together for the gospel.

2 Why was it important that the Philippians (and we) "stand firm in one spirit"?

_____

_____

_____

3 Why was it important that they (and we) "contend as one man for the faith of the gospel"?

_____

_____

_____

4 Paul and the Philippian church faced opposition because they were "contending", or fighting, for the gospel (verses 28-30). Why do you think the gospel causes opposition?

_____

_____

_____

BIBLE WORDS

v27 conduct. Behave.

v27 a manner. A way of doing or being.

v27 worthy. Honouring.

v27 in my absence. When I am not with you.

v27 contending. Struggling.

v27 oppose. Disagree with; try to stop.

v28 sign. Signal or symbol.

v29 granted. Given.

2v1 encouragement. Confidence, support, strength.

2v1 fellowship. Partnership.

2v1 tenderness and compassion. Kindness, love and concern.

2v3 selfish ambition. Wanting to be better than other people.

2v3 vain conceit. Stupid pride (pride = thinking you are better or more clever than others).

2v3 humility. The opposite of pride (see above).

5 What advice does Paul give the Philippians (and us) to help them as they face opposition?

6 Sometimes people say that if you become a Christian, you will be wealthy and healthy. What does Paul teach in verses 29-30 about the Christian life?

Read Philippians 2:1-11

7 Paul uses the word "if" four times in verse 1. What four things should make the Philippians "one in spirit and purpose"?

BIBLE WORDS

2v5 attitude. Way of thinking or feeling (about something).

2v6 equality with. Being the same as.

2v6 grasped. Held on to.

2v7 the very nature of. The form of.

2v9 exalted. Raised up; lifted up and honoured.

2v11 every tongue. Every person.

2v11 confess. Say publicly.

15

8 Read verses 3 & 4. How should Christians treat each other if they are one in spirit and purpose?

• What stops us from doing this?

9 If you "look to the interests of others", what will you do?

10 Whose example should we be following (verse 5)? Why?

■ *Read Philippians 2:1-11 again. Use these verses to help you to pray.*

THINGS TO PRAY FOR

MEMORY VERSE

"Your attitude should be the same as that of Christ Jesus."

Philippians 2:5

Philippians 2:5-18

How should I live for Christ?

Week 4

■ Which do you think is more important? To tell people the gospel or to live a godly life? Why?

_____

_____

_____

Read aloud Philippians 2:5-18

Read the verses again. Are there any words you do not understand? Look at the Bible words list on the next page to help you.

Read Philippians 2:5-11

Paul is telling his readers how they should live as disciples, following the example of Jesus.

1 What do verses 6-7 tell us about the identity of Jesus – who is he?

_____

_____

SUMMARY OF WEEKS 1-3

◁ Paul wrote this letter to help his readers keep going as Christians.

◁ Paul was confident that God would finish the work of salvation he began in them.

◁ The most important thing in Paul's life was that people were hearing about Jesus.

◁ Paul teaches the Philippians (and us) that: "To live is Christ and to die is gain." (1:21)

◁ We need to stay sure of what we believe and work together for the gospel. This will help us when we face opposition.

◁ God is at work in our lives changing us on the inside. These "inside changes" should lead to "outside changes" in the way Christians live and work together, and fight for the same things. Our attitude should be like Jesus.

17

2 Verse 8 tells us that Jesus humbled himself. How did he humble himself (verses 7-8)?

Jesus' death on a cross was not the end. Three days later God brought Jesus back to life.

3 What happened after Jesus came back to life (verse 9)?

- What is the result of this (verses 10-11)?

4 _Verses 5-11 show Jesus both as God and as our Servant King. He chose to be born as a human being so that he could die on a cross in our place._

- How does this make you feel?

- How should we respond? (See verse 5.)

BIBLE WORDS

v5 attitude. Way of thinking or feeling (about something).

v6 equality with. Being the same as.

v6 grasped. Held on to.

v7 the very nature of. The form of.

v9 exalted. Raised up; lifted up and honoured.

v11 every tongue. Every person.

v11 confess. Say publicly.

v12 in my presence. When I am with you.

v12 trembling. Shaking because you are afraid.

v15 blameless and pure. Someone who does not think wrong things or do wrong things.

v15 without fault. Without anything wrong.

v15 crooked and depraved. Sinful and evil.

v16 the word of life. The message about Jesus (the gospel).

Read Philippians 2:12-13

We have seen that when you become a Christian, God starts to change you on the inside. This inside change is shown by outside changes in our lives.

5 What does Paul tell the Philippian Christians to do in verse 12?

_____

_____

- Why do you think Paul describes this as continuing to "work out your salvation"?

_____

_____

6 Why must we do this with "fear and trembling"?

_____

_____

7 Look at verse 13. What is God doing while we are working out our salvation? How does that make you feel?

_____

_____

BIBLE WORDS

- **v16 boast.** Gladly tell everyone.
- **v16 the day of Christ.** The day when Jesus Christ will return to judge the world.
- **v16 run or labour.** Work hard.
- **v17 drink offering.** A drink offering = an Old Testament offering (a gift to God) of wine or water.
- **v17 sacrifice.** An offering to God. Chosen animals were sacrificed (killed as a gift to God). Sometimes in the Old Testament, a drink offering was poured on top of the sacrifice.

19

Read Philippians 2:14–18

8 Earlier in his letter Paul encouraged us to "conduct yourselves in a manner worthy of the gospel of Christ" (Philippians 1:27). In 2:14-16 what kind of behaviour is worthy of the gospel?

9 How should we "shine like stars"? Why?

10 Discuss the opening question again: Which do you think is more important – to tell people the gospel or to live a godly life among them? How does today's passage help you to answer this question?

■ *Pray for each other, asking God to change you to become more and more like Jesus, shining like stars among your family, friends and community.*

In Philippians 2:19-30 Paul gives two examples of people who were known to the Philippians and who showed the same attitude as Jesus. They are Timothy, who was servant-hearted, and Epaphroditus, who risked his life to help Paul. There is a short additional Bible-study about these two men on pages 37-38.

THINGS TO PRAY FOR

MEMORY VERSE

"Shine like stars in the universe as you hold out the word of life."

Philippians 2:15-16

Philippians 3:1-9

Can I be good enough for God?

Week 5

■ **What do people today think will make them good enough for God?**

_____

_____

_____

Read aloud Philippians 3:1-9

Read the verses again. Are there any words you do not understand? Look at the Bible words list on the next page to help you.

Read Philippians 3:1-3

1 From the outside, the situation looked bad for the Philippian Christians. Look back over chapters 1 & 2. What difficulties were the Philippians facing?

_____

_____

SUMMARY OF WEEKS 1-4

- Paul wrote this letter to help his readers keep going as Christians.

- Paul was confident that God would finish the work of salvation he began in them.

- The most important thing in Paul's life was that people were hearing about Jesus.

- Paul teaches the Philippians (and us) that: "To live is Christ and to die is gain." (1:21)

- We need to stay sure of what we believe and work together for the gospel. This will help us when we face opposition.

- God is at work in our lives changing both our thoughts and actions, making us more like Jesus.

- As disciples, we should behave differently to those around us – "shining like stars" as we point them to Jesus (2:15-16).

Even though the Philippians were facing opposition, Paul tells them to rejoice!

2 From what we have already seen in Paul's letter, why should they rejoice?

_____

_____

3 Rejoicing in all that Christ had done for them would protect them from another problem. What danger did they face (verses 2-3)?

_____

_____

• How will rejoicing in the Lord protect us from the same problem?

_____

_____

4 What three things show that someone truly belongs to Christ (verse 3)?

_____

_____

_____

BIBLE WORDS

v1 safeguard for you. A way to keep you safe.

v2 mutilators of the flesh. Those people who practise circumcision (see below) in order to get right with God.

v3 circumcision. Cutting off a small piece of skin from the penis. For Jewish people, circumcision is an outward sign showing that the man belongs to God's people. But God sent Jesus so that both Jews and non-Jews can become his people. Now the sign that someone is one of God's people is faith in Jesus and the Holy Spirit in their life, not physical circumcision.

v3 put no confidence in the flesh. Do not trust in things we do (like circumcision) to make us right with God.

v5 on the eighth day. At eight days old.

v5 tribe of Benjamin. All Jews came from one of 12 tribes (family groups). Benjamin was one of only two tribes that kept following God.

Read Philippians 3:4-9

5 Paul tells us how good he was as a religious Jew. What evidence does he give?

6 What does Paul think of his religious background and efforts? Do you find that surprising?

Paul knows that keeping religious rules will never make people good enough for God. It is not just useless – it is also harmful.

7 What makes us right with God?

8 Why do you think Paul uses such insulting language: "dogs" (verse 2), "rubbish" (verse 8)?

BIBLE WORDS

- **v5 Hebrew.** Another word for Jew.
- **v5 Pharisee.** A group of Jews who followed religious rules and customs very strictly.
- **v6 zeal.** Enthusiasm or passion for a belief or idea.
- **v6 persecuting.** Oppressing, treating badly.
- **v6 legalistic righteousness.** Keeping the Law of Moses.
- **v8 surpassing.** Exceptional, extraordinary.
- **v8-9 gain Christ and be found in him.** Know Christ and belong to him.

23

9 Before you became a Christian, what things did you rely on to make you right with God?

10 What things can you be tempted to rely on, in addition to your faith in Jesus?

11 Imagine you have a friend who tells you that they are not good enough for God. What would you say to them?

12 How can we help each other to keep trusting in Jesus, and not to trust in anything else?

- *Praise God that Jesus saves you when keeping religious rules can't.*
- *Pray that you will rejoice in the gospel.*
- *Pray that you will be alert for those who try to add things to the gospel.*
- *Pray for anyone in your group whose family or friends believe that keeping religious rules makes them good enough for God.*

THINGS TO PRAY FOR

MEMORY VERSE

"Not having a righteousness of my own that comes from the law, but that which is through faith in Christ – the righteousness that comes from God and is by faith."

Philippians 3:9

Philippians 3:10 – 4:1

How can I know Christ better?

Week 6

■ What is the difference between knowing about someone and knowing them as a friend? List some ways you can get to know someone better.

_____

_____

_____

Read aloud Philippians 3:10 – 4:1

Read the verses again. Are there any words you do not understand? Look at the Bible words list on the next page to help you.

Read Philippians 3:10-14

1 Are you surprised that Paul says that he wants to know Christ? Why?

_____

_____

SUMMARY OF WEEKS 1-5

- Paul wrote this letter to help his readers keep going as Christians.
- Paul was confident that God would finish the work of salvation he began in them.
- The most important thing in Paul's life was that people were hearing about Jesus.
- Paul teaches the Philippians (and us) that: "To live is Christ and to die is gain." (1:21)
- We need to stay sure of what we believe and work together for the gospel.
- Our attitude should be like Jesus, as we shine like stars to those around us.
- Paul knew that keeping religious rules was worthless. It is faith in Christ alone that makes a person right with God.

25

*Knowing Christ is much more than just knowing **about** him. Paul has already said that Christians are "in Christ" (see 1:1) and "united with Christ" (2:1).*

2 How does Paul describe the cost of knowing Christ (verses 10-11)?

3 What comforts come from knowing Christ (verses 10-11)?

Read Philippians 3:12–16

4 What is the "one thing" that Paul does (verses 12-14)?

BIBLE WORDS

v11 attain to the resurrection. To rise to life after I die.

v12 press on. Keep going.

v13 straining. Working hard to keep going.

v15 mature. Grown up.

v16 live up to. Live in a way that shows.

v16 attained. Achieved, gained.

v17 live according to the pattern we gave you. Live in the way we showed or taught you.

v19 their destiny. Their future after death.

v19 their glory is in their shame. They are proud of the sinful things that they do.

v20 citizenship. Home.

v20 eagerly await. Keenly wait for.

v21 transform. Completely change.

v21 lowly. Nothing special.

5 Do you think a Christian can ever be perfect?

6 So what does it mean to be a "mature believer" (verse 15)?

Read Philippians 3:17 – 4:1

7 Paul says there are only two ways to live. What are they?

8 Where do these two ways lead?

BIBLE WORDS

v21 glorious. Wonderful.

4v1 stand firm in the Lord. Don't let anything take you away from the Lord.

9 What does it mean to be a citizen of heaven?

10 Paul says that our "citizenship is in heaven" and that Christ will return. How will these facts help us to press on?

11 From Philippians chapter 3 can you summarise how we can "stand firm in the Lord" (4:1)?

- *Thank God that you have been saved by Christ and so you can eagerly wait for his return.*
- *Ask God to help you to press on as a disciple of Jesus.*
- *Pray for any you know whose "destiny is destruction" (3:19).*
- *Ask God to help you stand firm in the Lord.*

THINGS TO PRAY FOR

MEMORY VERSE

"I want to know Christ and the power of his resurrection and the fellowship of sharing in his sufferings."

Philippians 3:10

Philippians 4:2-9

How can I rejoice in Christ?

Week 7

■ **What things make you worry? What do you do when you are anxious?**

_____

_____

_____

Read aloud Philippians 4:2-9

Read the verses again. Are there any words you do not understand?
Look at the Bible words list on the next page to help you.

Read Philippians 4:2-3

1 What encouraging things do verses 2-3 tell us about the two women Euodia and Syntyche?

_____

_____

SUMMARY OF WEEKS 1-6

- Paul wrote this letter to help his readers keep going as Christians. He was confident that God would finish the work of salvation he began in them.

- The most important thing in Paul's life was that people were hearing about Jesus.

- Paul teaches the Philippians (and us) that: "To live is Christ and to die is gain." (1:21)

- We need to stay sure of what we believe and work together for the gospel.

- Our attitude should be like Jesus, as we shine like stars to those around us.

- It is faith in Christ alone that makes a person right with God.

- We need to press on as disciples of Jesus and stand firm in the Lord.

Paul doesn't get involved in the detail of the disagreement between the two women. Instead, he tells them that they must "agree with each other in the Lord" (verse 2).

2 What do you think it means to agree in the Lord?

_____

_____

- How can we help each other do that (like the "loyal yokefellow" in verse 3)?

_____

_____

Read Philippians 4:4–7

3 Paul tells us to "rejoice in the Lord always". Do you think this is possible? Why or why not?

_____

_____

4 What should we do as Christians when we are feeling worried?

_____

_____

BIBLE WORDS

v2 plead. Ask for something that you want very much.

v3 loyal yokefellow. True friend.

v3 contended. Worked hard, struggled.

v3 in the cause of the gospel. For the gospel.

v3 the book of life. A picture used in the Bible to talk about the list of people who God has chosen and saved through Jesus Christ.

v4 rejoice in. Find joy in, take delight in.

v5 evident to all. Seen by everyone.

v6 anxious. Worried.

v6 petition. Humbly asking for something.

v6 your requests. What you are asking for.

v7 transcends. Is far beyond.

v7 guard. Keep safe.

5 How do these things help us not to be anxious?

6 What will be the result if we obey verses 4-6? (See verse 7.)

Read Philippians 4:8-9

7 What should we spend our time thinking about?

8 Write down the opposites of the words Paul uses in verse 8. How would you be different if you spent time thinking about these things?

BIBLE WORDS

v8 noble. Good.

v8 admirable. Something you should admire (respect).

v9 put it into practice. Do it.

Our minds are filled with the things we watch, read, do and listen to: TV, internet sites, magazines, books, computer games and music.

9 So how can we encourage each other to fill our minds with things that are noble, right, pure etc? Give practical answers.

_____

_____

10 What is the command in verse 9 and what is promised?

_____

_____

In verses 4-9, Paul has told us to agree in the Lord, rejoice in the Lord, pray to the Lord and think in a way that pleases the Lord.

11 What will you find most difficult about doing what Paul tells us?

_____

_____

■ ***Pray for each other now.***

THINGS TO PRAY FOR

MEMORY VERSE

"Do not be anxious about anything, but in everything, by prayer and petition, with thanksgiving, present your requests to God."

Philippians 4:6

Philippians 4:10-23

How can I be content in Christ?

Week 8

■ "My life would be great if only..."
How would people you know finish that sentence? How would you finish it?

___

___

Read aloud Philippians 4:10-23

Read the verses again. Are there any words you do not understand?
Look at the Bible words list on the next page to help you.

Read Philippians 4:10-13

Paul wrote this letter from prison. We know from the rest of the Bible that Paul had known times of comfort and times of great trouble.

1 What situations does Paul list in verse 12?

___

___

> **SUMMARY OF WEEKS 1-7**
>
> ◁ Paul's letter helps us keep going as Christians. We can be confident that God will finish the work he has begun in us.
>
> ◁ The most important thing is that people are hearing about Jesus. We need to stay sure of what we believe and work together for the gospel.
>
> ◁ "To live is Christ and to die is gain." (1:21)
>
> ◁ Our attitude should be like Jesus, as we shine like stars to those around us.
>
> ◁ It is faith in Christ alone that makes a person right with God.
>
> ◁ We need to press on as disciples of Jesus and stand firm in the Lord.
>
> ◁ As disciples, we should agree in the Lord, rejoice in the Lord, pray to the Lord and think in a way that pleases the Lord.

2 Why do you think it is important to be content whether we are rich or poor?

3 What is the secret of being content?

4 How can we learn to be content in our circumstances?

5 Does verse 13 mean that Paul has a super-human ability to do anything? If not, what does he mean?

BIBLE WORDS

v10 renewed. Started again.

v10 concern. Take an interest in.

v11 I am in need. I don't have the things that I need.

v11 content. Satisfied.

v11 circumstances. Situation.

v12 to have plenty. To have even more than I need.

v12 in want. Poor.

v15 moreover. Also.

v15 in the early days. Near the beginning.

v15 acquaintance with the gospel. Personal knowledge of the gospel.

v15 set out. Left.

v15 Macedonia. Philippi was in Macedonia, part of ancient Greece.

v15 shared with. Involved with, helped.

v15 Thessalonica. Another city in Macedonia.

v16 aid. Help.

Read Philippians 4:14-19

Although Paul is content in prison, he is also grateful for the gift the Philippian Christians sent to him.

6 How does Paul describe their giving in verses 14 and 18?

7 What is the pattern of giving that we see in these verses and how can we follow it? (See also verses 10-11.)

8 Read verse 19. Does this mean that Christians will never be poor? Why or why not?

BIBLE WORDS

v17 credited. Added.

v18 I am amply supplied. I have everything I need.

v18 fragrant. Sweet smelling, pleasing.

v18 acceptable sacrifice. A gift to God that pleases him.

v19 according to. In proportion to.

v19 glorious. Wonderful.

v22 Caesar's household. The people who live and work in Caesar's house.

v22 Amen. A Hebrew word which means "certainly" or "so be it".

Read Philippians 4:20–23

9 What is so encouraging about the way Paul ends his letter – especially verse 22?

10 Tell the rest of the group one thing that has helped you grow as a disciple as you have studied Philippians together.

- *Ask God to help you to learn the secret of being content in every situation.*
- *Pray about your giving.*
- *Give thanks for the things that people have said have helped them to grow as disciples.*

THINGS TO PRAY FOR

MEMORY VERSE

"I have learned the secret of being content in any and every situation."

Philippians 4:12

Philippians 2:19–30

An example to follow?

■ Who did you want to be like when you were a child? Why was that person, or their job, attractive to you?

_____

_____

Read aloud Philippians 2:19–30

Read the verses again. Are there any words you do not understand? Look at the Bible words list on this page to help you.

Read Philippians 2:19–24

Paul longs to visit the Philippian Christians again, to see for himself how they are getting on. But he is in prison, so he is hoping to send two of his friends, Timothy and Epaphroditus, to them.

1 What do we learn about Timothy and what matters to him from these verses?

_____

_____

Extra

BIBLE WORDS

v19 be cheered. Be made happy.

v20 takes a genuine interest in your welfare. Truly cares about how well you are doing.

v21 looks out for. Is interested in.

v22 proved himself. Shown that he is good.

v26 distressed. Very sad and worried.

v27 to spare me sorrow upon sorrow. To keep me from lots of sadness.

v28 I am … eager. I want very much.

v30 risking his life. He was in danger of dying.

2 What kind of relationship does Paul have with Timothy?

Read Philippians 2:25–30 and 4:18

3 Who was Epaphroditus and what happened to him?

4 Why do you think Paul encourages the Philippian Christians to welcome Epaphroditus back?

5 In what three ways does Paul describe Epaphroditus in verse 25? What do they teach us about the Christian life?

6 Timothy and Epaphroditus are both young Christians, but Paul still uses them as examples to follow. How can we be examples to others?

- *Thank God for the examples of Paul, Timothy and Epaphroditus.*
- *Pray for each other and ask God to help you to be examples to others.*

THINGS TO PRAY FOR

Notes

Notes